anythink

I Want to Be a VELOCIRAPTOR

by Thomas Kingsley Troupe

illustrated by Jomike Tejido

PICTURE WINDOW BOOKS
a capstone imprint

Nicole and I watched the girls' soccer team. It was a close game and the crowd was going wild.

"Looks like they're having fun out there," Nicole said. A second later, the Valley Creek Velociraptors scored. "Don't you think, Valerie?"

"Yeah," I said, suddenly wishing I had joined the team.

| Valley Creek Velociraptors | 1 |
| Sunny Hill Scorpions | 1 |

I imagined running down the field, dribbling and driving toward the goal. People would be cheering for me! When our team scored again, we all stood up.

"I want to be a Velociraptor!" I shouted. "Then I'll be great at soccer too!"

I'm not sure why, but the moment I said those words, I turned into a REAL Velociraptor! I ran onto the field. People shouted and pointed at me.

I scrambled through the players fleeing from the field. I ducked low and ran beneath their legs. I had to get out of there. I was causing too much trouble!

Once I was off the field, I knew I was somewhere different. The air was hot and there was sand everywhere. Was I in a desert? The air felt dry and dusty.

A few Velociraptors ran past me. One of them stopped. She cocked her head like a bird.

"Um, hi," I said. My voice felt squeaky, almost like I'd squawked.

PREHISTORIC DINO-BIRDS! Velociraptors lived during the Cretaceous Period, which spanned 145.5 to 65.5 million years ago. Other dinosaur superstars living during this period included: Triceratops, Stegoceras, Spinosaurus, and Tyrannosaurus rex.

"I'm Sue," the Velociraptor said. "You're not from around here, are you?"

"I'm Valerie," I said. She smiled, and I saw she had about 30 sharp teeth in her mouth.

DINOSAURS OF A FEATHER FLOCK TOGETHER? Scientists know Velociraptors had feathers all over their bodies. But they aren't sure exactly what the feathers looked like or what color they were.

The sand felt hot beneath my feet, so I lifted my foot. I glanced from my legs to Sue's legs. Like mine, they were thin, almost like turkey legs. Like Sue, I also had a tail! It was stiff and I couldn't wag it like my dog, Zeke, wagged his back home.

"Come with us," Sue said. "We're going to hunt for food."
Before I could say anything, Sue was gone. I ran after her, feeling the hot wind in my feathers. Was I a bird or a dinosaur?
I looked ahead to where the others were. My eyes were awesome! They gave me binocular vision. It felt like I could see for miles!

I slowed down near a small creek. Three other Velociraptors stood near some strange plants. A Protoceratops drank water from a stream.

"Perfect," the herd leader said. "He'll never know what hit him!"

I stared down at the herd's feet, then mine. The middle toe on each foot had a giant claw. The claws looked like hook-shaped blades!

"Are you ready?" Sue asked me. I wasn't sure what to do. A second later, the Velociraptors ran at the poor Protoceratops.

I stayed behind as they attacked the little beast. I couldn't watch!

"What happened to you?" Sue asked.

"I was watching for attackers," I said, making up a story.

"Good thinking," Sue said. "We're tough little creatures, but any big meat-eaters could gobble us right up."

WATCH YOUR FEET! Scientists think Velociraptors used their feet to attack prey. They would kick and slash at their victims, and then they would wait for them to die from the wounds. Scientists also think Velociraptors used their talons to hold prey and keep it from escaping.

9

"Come get something to eat," Sue said, "before it's gone!"
I walked through the bushes. The other Velociraptors didn't
look up from their meat. They ate like it was their last meal.

"I'm not too hungry," I said. But when a bug buzzed nearby, I tracked it with my eyes. Without thinking, I quickly caught it in my mouth and ate it. Ugh! What was I doing?

Once the Protoceratops meat was gone, the other Velociraptors poked around the bushes. Everyone was still hungry.

BON APPÉTIT! A Velociraptor couldn't be too picky about what it ate. It had to survive on reptiles, bugs, small dinosaurs, and mammals.

All of the Velociraptors started getting upset. No one could find more food to eat. I saw one of them bite another. Then that one bit a third who was too close to him.

Before I knew it, all of them were attacking each other.

"I'm out of here," I squawked, and ran off into the desert. I didn't want to get into a fight . . . or get eaten!

I could hear something running behind me. Were the Velociraptors coming after me? I turned my head on my long neck. It was Sue. "Wait up!" she called. She didn't look angry, so I slowed down.

"Sorry about that," Sue said. "We're not very good at working together for long. We Velociraptors are used to being by ourselves."

CAN'T WE ALL JUST GET ALONG? Some scientists think Velociraptors might have liked to hunt and roam in packs . . . but not always. One set of Velociraptor fossils showed a fatal bite from another Velociraptor.

When we were far away from the other Velociraptors, we slowed down. Over near some sand dunes, I saw a mama Velociraptor. She was watching over a nest of small eggs in the ground.

The mom saw us and raised her feathers.

"Wow," I said. "Aren't there any friendly Velociraptors?"

"Don't take it so hard," Sue said. "Everyone's hungry these days. She probably thinks you're after her eggs . . ."

". . . or her babies."

I watched a little Velociraptor break out of its shell. It really looked like a baby bird, and it made small crying sounds.

Mama Velociraptor gave the baby some mashed up meat to eat.

UGLY BUT CUTE! Fossilized skulls show that baby Velociraptors had much shorter snouts and bigger eyes than adults. Scientists think mama Velociraptors watched over their babies after they hatched.

Sue and I moved along, leaving the mama and her babies alone. After walking a while, we saw older, skinnier Velociraptors searching for food. They looked hungry, but there wasn't much to eat.

"How long can Velociraptors survive like this?" I asked.

"Hard to say," Sue said sadly. "When there was more food, we could live up to 20 years. But lately the plant-eaters have been running out of food. If they can't eat, we can't eat."

I looked around at the huge desert all around us. I only
saw a few places where there were plants or water.

I wondered where in the world we were. For all I knew,
I was on the other side of the world from my house—millions
of years and a million miles away!

FOSSIL FINDS! Velociraptor fossils
have been discovered in the Gobi Desert.
This desert stretches across southern
Mongolia and parts of Northern China.

Gobi Desert

We moved further into the desert. Just about everywhere I looked, sick Velociraptors were moving slowly.

"It's not looking good for us," Sue said. "It seems like none of us can get enough to eat anymore."

Up in the sky, I saw colorful streaks. It looked like things were falling to Earth. I turned to see a giant, flaming rock heading my way! Just before it hit . . .

WHAT HAPPENED TO THE DINOS? Scientists aren't really sure how Velociraptors or any dinosaurs became extinct. Some think volcanoes, disease, or even giant meteorites led to them dying out.

. . . I was back at the soccer field. I put my hands up and caught a loose ball from the game, just in time!

"Wow!" Nicole said. "You should totally join the team as a goal keeper next year."

"I think I will," I said. I threw the ball back to the referee. Our team was down by one point. "It looks like the Velociraptors could use the help!"

MORE ABOUT VELOCIRAPTOR

The name Velociraptor means "speedy thief."

In 1971 fossils of a Velociraptor and a Protoceratops were found in the Gobi Desert. The two appeared to be locked in battle when they were buried alive in a sandstorm.

A Velociraptor's feathers may have had several uses. They were likely used to attract mates and maintain body temperature. They also may have shielded eggs from prey and helped generate speed when running uphill.

Velociraptor was roughly the size of a small turkey. It stood about 3 feet (1 meter) tall, and was about 6.8 feet (2.07 m) long. It weighed about 30 pounds (13.6 kilograms).

Velociraptor had a large skull compared to its small body. Scientists think Velociraptor's large brain made it one of the more intelligent dinosaurs.

The hook-shaped claw on a Velociraptor's foot was probably used to hold prey in place like a hawk or falcon.

GLOSSARY

extinct—no longer living; an extinct animal is one that has died out, with no more of its kind

fatal—causing death

flock—to gather in a crowd

fossil—the remains or traces of an animal or a plant, preserved as rock

herd—a large group of animals that lives or moves together

mammal—a warm-blooded animal that breathes air; mammals have hair or fur; female mammals feed milk to their young

meteorite—a piece of meteor that falls all the way to the ground

prey—an animal hunted by another animal for food

reptile—a cold-blooded animal that breathes air and has a backbone; most reptiles have scales

squawk—to make a loud, harsh screech

talon—a long, sharp claw

READ MORE

Raymond, Jayne. *Meet Velociraptor.* The Age of DInosaurs. New York: Cavendish Square, 2015.

Rissman, Rebecca. *Velociraptor and Other Raptors.* Dinosaur Fact Dig. North Mankato, Minn.: Captstone Press, 2016.

West, David. *Dinosaurs of the Cretaceous.* Mankato, Minn.: Smart Apple Media, 2015.

INTERNET SITES

FactHound offers a safe, fun way to find internet sites related to this book. All of the sites on FactHound have been researched by our staff.

Here's all you do:
Visit *www.facthound.com*
Type in this code: 9781479587698

Super-cool stuff!

Check out projects, games and lots more at
www.capstonekids.com

INDEX

BOOKS IN THE SERIES

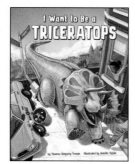
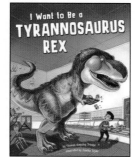
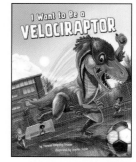

Dedication: To Jake, who really wishes he was a bird so he can fly . . . but runs like a Velociraptor!

Thanks to our adviser for his expertise, research, and advice:
Mathew J. Wedel, PhD
Associate Professor
Western University of Health Services

Editors: Christopher Harbo and Anna Butzer
Designer: Sarah Bennett
Art Director: Ashlee Suker
Production Specialist: Kathy McColley

The illustrations in this book were planned with pencil on paper and finished with digital paints.

Picture Window Books are published by Capstone, 1710 Roe Crest Drive, North Mankato, Minnesota 56003
www.capstonepub.com

Library of Congress Cataloging-in-Publication Data
Catalogue-in-publication information is on file with the Library of Congress.

ISBN 978-1-4795-8769-8 (library binding)
ISBN 978-1-4795-8773-5 (eBook PDF)

Summary: Follows a young girl as she transforms into a Velociraptor and experiences life from a dinosaur's perspective.

Printed and bound in the USA.
009685F16